# Family Devotional

## Joseph Borowitz

Copyright © 2019 by Joseph Borowitz

ISBN-10: **1642540765**
ISBN-13: 9781642540765

All rights reserved. No part of this book may be reproduced or transmitted in any form or by any means, electronic or mechanical, including photocopying, recording, or by any information storage and retrieval system, without permission in writing from the copyright owner.

Print information available on the last page

# CONTENTS

Chapter 1   CREATION .................................................................................. 2

Chapter 2   FAMILIES: GOD'S IDEA ............................................................. 4

Chapter 3   THE HOLY FAMILY .................................................................... 6

Chapter 4   JESUS CAME TO SHOW GOD TO US ..................................... 8

Chapter 5   BAPTISM ................................................................................... 10

Chapter 6   GO TO CHURCH ....................................................................... 12

Chapter 7   PRAYER .................................................................................... 14

Chapter 8   RESURRECTION ...................................................................... 16

Chapter 9   PENTECOST ............................................................................. 18

Chapter 10   PEACEMAKERS ..................................................................... 20

Chapter 11   GOOD SAMARITAN ............................................................... 24

Chapter 12   LABORERS IN THE VINEYARD ........................................... 26

Chapter 13   EACH PERSON NEEDS A DEEP SPIRITUALITY ............... 28

Chapter 14   PRODIGAL SON ..................................................................... 30

Chapter 15   GOD RULES THE NATIONS ................................................. 32

Chapter 16   DRUGS AND FAMILIES ........................................................ 34

Chapter 17   FAMILIES AND MENTAL ILLNESS .................................... 38

Chapter 18   IMPORTANCE OF SMALL PRAYER GROUPS ................... 42

# CHAPTER 1

# CREATION

How do we know there is a God? You can't see Him or touch Him or hear Him. But the bible tells us He is the creator of all things including you and I. The stars in the heavens, the beautiful mountains and oceans were all created by Him. The bible tells us that the greatest thing God created is humans. Even though some animals are stronger and can run faster than us, and some can fly or live deep within the ocean, still men are greater. Why is this? It's because we are the only ones who can understand godly things and appreciate the power of God. You usually don't see any dogs or cats or horses in church. They wouldn't know what's going on.

Yet God takes care of us all. We humans farm and harvest all kinds of foods. We build nice homes and make fancy cars. We think we do all this ourselves but without God's help none of this would be possible. God also takes care of the animals. You never see squirrels or rabbits in grocery stores, yet the squirrels and rabbits in our neighborhoods look very healthy. Somebody is taking care of them. Thank you God for your loving kindness to all of creation.

## DISCUSSION QUESTIONS

Name some animals that can run faster than people.
Name some animals that are stronger than men.
Name some animals that can jump higher than men.
Name some animals that can climb trees faster than men.

# CHAPTER 2
# FAMILIES: GOD'S IDEA

In Genesis 2:18 the first book of the bible, it says "It is not good for men to be alone. I will make a helper for him". Then God created women to be a helper for men." Therefore men and women were created for one another. The husband and wife together are able to have children and to form a family. So families were God's idea.

God told the prophet Abraham that he was to be the Father of a great nation, and that all families of earth would be blessed through Abraham. He had twelve grandsons who established the twelve tribes of Israel.

All of Jesus' Apostles were descendants of Abraham. King David was of the Tribe of Judah and Mary, the mother of Jesus was a descendent of King David. St. Paul was of the Tribe of Benjamin, another one of Abraham's grandsons. Our families have inherited much of the bible and much of the wisdom of Christianity from the Jewish people. We are truly blessed because of the faith of Abraham and his descendants.

If we have good strong families in a church, we have a good church. If we have good strong families in a city, we have a good strong city. God is the one who put each of us in a loving family so we would each receive the care and attention we needed to grow into healthy people. He invented love and faithfulness so that men and women would be attracted to one another and together they would become dedicated mothers and fathers. This was God's plan to form a really good society.

Families teach us important lessons;

To love one another
To be honest
To respect authority
To eat and dress properly
To exercise and get good sleep
To brush our teeth and keep our rooms neat

# CHAPTER 3
# THE HOLY FAMILY

Human families are not perfect, even though people try their best. There's always something lacking. But the Holy Family (Jesus, Mary and Joseph) was absolutely perfect. How could this be since Jesus was the Son of God and Creator of the Universe? How could He obey Mary and Joseph who were only human? Seems to me that God had to make sure that Jesus would be well prepared for the job He had to do. So Mary and Joseph were closely guided by God the Father and by the Holy Spirit so that when his parents spoke to Jesus it was all motivated by godly authority.

When I was in Jerusalem, they pointed out the place where Mary lived when she was a little girl. It was not far from the temple. They told us that Mary's mother, St. Ann took her daughter to be educated by the Rabbis in the temple. So Mary could read and write. Few people could do this in those days. The men Jesus chose to be Apostles could not read or write, with the possible exception of St Matthew. That's probably why God had to single out St. Paul, an educated man to help start the new church. Also Mary took Jesus to the temple in Nazareth to learn to read and write. We know that Jesus could read because He did the reading in the temple after He started His earthly ministry.

The Holy Family is a good example for other families to follow. St. Paul tells us in Colossians 3:12-14, that families need to be holy, kind, humble, merciful, meek bearing with one another and above all. families need to love and forgive others. The fourth commandment must have been special to Jesus "Honor your Father and your Mother".

# CHAPTER 4
# JESUS CAME TO SHOW GOD TO US

Most of us first hear about God from our families. We hear stories about Jesus, the Son of God and about the miraculous things He did while He was here on earth. He healed all the sick people who came to him. He even raised people from the dead. He also shared with us powerful stories called parables which tell us how to live good lives in this complicated world.

Moses had already given the Jews the Ten Commandments, but that wasn't enough. They needed to have a good example to follow. They needed someone who was perfect, without sin, someone who was treated terribly and still was able to forgive. That's why God sent Jesus, to be an example of a truly good and holy person. Jesus was the Son of God! He is a member of the Holy Trinity.

## DISCUSSION QUESTIONS

Can you think of anything Jesus did that was unfair?
Did Jesus ever put himself first ahead of other people?
Did Jesus ever say no to people who asked him for help?
Did Jesus ever mistreat his Mother or his foster Father?
What do they mean when they say Jesus was fully human and fully divine.

# CHAPTER 5

# BAPTISM

Usually our parents have us baptized when we're little babies. We don't understand what's happening. But this is an important event bringing us into full membership in the church that Jesus came to establish. Baptism in one Christian denomination is valid in all Christian churches. It doesn't have to be repeated even if we start attending another denomination. Some churches delay baptism till the child is a teenager or older so that they can understand more what it's all about.

Baptism forgives us from all sin and makes us clean so that we can be close to God who is without sin. As it says in the bible, what fellowship does light have with darkness? How can we who are imperfect, fellowship with a perfect God? We absolutely need the sacrament of baptism.

Jesus was baptized in the Jordan River by John the Baptist. Why did He need to be baptized? He never committed any sin. He was the Son of God, the second person of the Blessed Trinity. Two reasons, maybe He needed more fellowship with the Holy Spirit as He began his mission on earth. Also a voice spoke when Jesus was baptized and said "This is my beloved Son in whom I am well pleased." Maybe this was an important announcement to all people that Jesus was the Son of God.

# CHAPTER 6
# GO TO CHURCH

At the Last Supper, Jesus took bread and broke it and told His apostles to eat it. Then He took wine and blessed it and told His apostles to drink it. Then He said to them "Do this in memory of me." He was really telling them to go to church and to consume the bread and wine because this bread and wine are transformed right there in church into the body and blood of Jesus himself. Then He told them unless you do this regularly you shall not have life within you!

So it's important for families to go to church and consume the Eucharist. It brings them together. We become one body in Christ as the nutrients are transformed into our own flesh. Also we feed our Spirits just as Jesus told us to do.

Humans are made of three parts, body, mind and spirit. Each part needs to be fed. We eat breakfast, lunch and dinner every day to feed our physical bodies. We learn new things daily to keep our minds nourished. Sometimes we forget about our spirits. We need to go to church regularly to keep our spirits fed with the Eucharist and with godly thoughts.

# CHAPTER 7

## PRAYER

St. Paul (Romans 12:12) tells us to pray all the time. Despite all the work we need to do, we need to pray constantly. How can we do this? One way is to make our work a prayer also. It takes an effort but it keeps us connected to God.

Some people try to tell you how to pray. Others say, just go ahead and pray anyway you want, but keep at it and keep working also.

Pray for your family, pray for your friends, pray for your teachers, your neighbors, your dog, and pray for yourselves. God already knows everything about you but He still wants to hear from you. Tell him your deepest feelings, your deepest hurts. Ask for His help.

Jesus himself taught us the "Our Father", a fine prayer. In it we ask for God's will to be done. Why do we need to do that? Won't His will be done whether we ask for it or not? One reason is that we need to be able to accept his will, once it is done. So this is an important part of this holy prayer.

Most importantly, pray for God's guidance in all that you do that you may be effective in building God's kingdom. Also don't forget to pray for your enemies that you can love them.

Remember the story of Jesus walking on the water? Peter asked Jesus if he could also walk on water. Jesus said "come". Peter did and was OK as long as he was thinking about Jesus but when he noticed the wind was strong, he began to sink. We need to keep our spiritual eyes on Jesus and pray all the time. Jesus asked Peter "Why did you doubt?" The power to walk on water

was given to Peter. He had it and was doing fine but then he doubted and began to sink. Doubts work against prayer.

There's a story about St. Teresa of Lisieux who died at the age of twenty four of tuberculosis. For most of her life she was a little girl. She imagined herself, a small child going up the stairs to see Jesus on the top of the staircase. She prayed her way up the steps making faltering, childish movements. Finally Jesus came down the steps, picked her up and carried her to the top. Like Teresa we need to make genuine efforts to keep going. And at some point, God will come down and rescue us and we will see the fruits of our labor.

# CHAPTER 8
# RESURRECTION

The apostle John in his first epistle said God sent His Son to be sacrificed so our sins could be forgiven. Some think that's awful. Why couldn't God just forgive us of all sin? God is a God of love and mercy and kindness, how could He allow His beloved Son to die on the cross? Why not just forgive everyone without having anyone die.

But this whole plan was agreed upon before the world began. Jesus agreed with it and probably said "That's Ok Father, I think it's a good idea and a powerful thing to be resurrected from the dead. Surely nobody on earth could ignore something like that."

We date our calendar from the time Jesus came to earth. He made a great impression here. He predicted He would die and rise again. If he had not risen from the dead, there would be no Christian Church. All His good deeds would be forgotten because He was not a truthful man. But He did rise from the dead to prove beyond a doubt that He was the Son of God.

Atonement for the sins of mankind is believed to come through Jesus' sacrifice on the cross. Revelation 1:5 says that Jesus loved us and washed us free from our sins with His own blood. Without the sacrifice of Jesus on the cross and His resurrection, there would be no atonement, no forgiveness of sins and no Christian Church.

# CHAPTER 9
# PENTECOST

Just before Jesus ascended into heaven from the Mount of Olives just outside of the walls of Jerusalem, He told His apostles to wait a few days in the City and pray for the anointing of the Holy Spirit. He had been in the Jerusalem area for forty days after His resurrection and had been seen by many people. However, the apostles were still afraid that the Jews might come and crucify them also. So Jesus told them that the Holy Spirit would come upon them and give them power and courage to share His teachings throughout the whole world. Then before their eyes, Jesus ascended into heaven.

When I was in Jerusalem, I visited the little Chapel of the Ascension built on the Mount of Olives. There is a footprint beside the Chapel, which is said to be the last footprint Jesus left on earth.

So the apostles did as Jesus said and waited there in Jerusalem for about 10 days. They were gathered in the Upper Room and had locked the doors because of their fear of the Jews. While they were praying, they felt a wind and tongues of fire appeared on each of their heads. It was the Holy Spirit that Jesus had told them to wait for. When they were filled with the Holy Spirit, they unlocked the doors and were no longer afraid. Then they went out into the streets where people had gathered. The apostles spoke to the crowds about all the miracles Jesus had performed. Even though the people there were from foreign countries and spoke different languages, they all understood what was said.

The apostles acted so boldly, the people thought they were drunk with new

wine. Peter stood up and said they were not drunk but explained that Jesus, whom they had crucified, was raised from the dead! And Jesus had passed His Spirit on to the apostles who were now telling everyone that God had made Jesus both Lord and Christ. They announced that a new age has begun, empowered by the Holy Spirit who dwells now in everyone who opens their hearts to receive. We also can trust Jesus to help us to open our hearts to receive the Holy Spirit with all His power, joy and peace.

# CHAPTER 10
# PEACEMAKERS

Let's mention someone who was a deeply spiritual man and brought great peace into the world. Mohandas Gandhi was born in India but at the age of 23 went to London, England to become a lawyer. Then he worked for 21 years in South Africa which was also under British control like his home country, India. He knew people in both of these British Colonies were not treated fairly. When he was 44 years old, he went home to help his own people become free.

Even though he was a devout Hindu, he read the bible and appreciated the teachings of Jesus, especially the beatitudes. He searched for the best way to work for justice for the poor and freedom for people not treated fairly.

Gandhi's spirituality brought him to respect and love all living things. People called him "Mahatma" which means someone with a great soul. He decided to obtain justice for the poor without violence or warfare. He prayed and fasted in the struggle for freedom. He taught his poor countrymen to treat others with kindness even when the British beat them or even killed them.

He became a leader of the Indian National Congress and dealt with the British always along peaceful lines even amid the chaos of WWII. The British finally approved the independence of India in 1947. People now respect Gandhi but in his efforts to attain independence, he was imprisoned several times and they mistreated him in any way they could.

In January 1948, Gandhi was on his way to speak at a Hindu prayer meeting and was shot by a man upset because Gandhi did not defend Muslims enough.

Gandhi won independence for his country, India. He used peaceful means and never hurt anyone. He prevented much bloodshed and finally brought freedom to his people. The beatitudes listed below were a source of faith and a guide for all the good that Gandhi accomplished.

Jesus wants us to be happy and also to share that happiness with all other people. Your parents and the rest of your family want you to be happy. God and your Pastor want you to be happy. To help us, Jesus gave us the beatitudes in Matthew 5:3-11 and Luke 6:21-29 which are summarized here. The word beatitude means happiness.

1. Blessed are the poor in spirit. When you know you need God and always put Him first in all you do in life, then you are happy.
2. Blessed are they who morn. When someone you love dies, you know they are in heaven and even though you are sad about their death, you have joy knowing that God is taking care of them.
3. Blessed are the meek. When you are humble and do what God wants you to do, you are happy. Some will tell you it's not good to be meek. We have to be aggressive and to be good salesmen and make a lot of money. Yet Jesus says blessed are the meek.
4. Blessed are they who want what is right. These are fair-minded people who want everyone to be happy even though they themselves may not be favored.
5. Blessed are the merciful. Those who can forgive and want the best for others are happy people.
6. Blessed are the clean of heart. People who are innocent and want the best for all other people are the happiest.
7. Blessed are the peacemakers. Happy people want everyone to love other people.

8. Blessed are those persecuted for righteousness. These people are happy when they've done good for others even though they suffered for it.
9. Blessed are you when men hate you and exclude you for the Son of Man's sake. Your reward will be great in heaven.
10. Blessed are those who love their enemies and who pray for those who despitefully use people.
11. Blessed are they who give to all those who ask of them.
12. Blessed are they who turn the other cheek.

# CHAPTER 11
# GOOD SAMARITAN

Jesus told a parable (a story usually easy to understand) about a man who traveled from Jerusalem to Jericho and was severely beaten and his money stolen. A Jewish priest walked by. Surely he would stop and help the man, but no, he passed by on the other side of the road. Then a Levite came by. Levites are people who clean and repair the temple. Surely he would do something good for the injured man, but no, he also walked on by. Then a Samaritan, a person disliked by Jews, noticed the man and helped him. He took him to a motel, bandaged his wounds, and paid for him to stay in the motel. Then Jesus asked the people which one did the right thing and they said the Samaritan.

This is an important parable showing that even though the Jews did not like the Samaritans, still this Samaritan helped the Jewish man at a time when he really needed it, and the Jewish priest and Levite did nothing. The Samaritan overcame any feelings of resentment toward himself by Jews, and did the right thing for the injured Jewish man.

1 John 4:16 says God is love. That's all inclusive. We need to love God, our neighbor (even if they are our enemies) and ourselves. It's like a three legged stool, if one of the legs falls off, the stool falls over.

# CHAPTER 12
# LABORERS IN THE VINEYARD

Another parable told by Jesus involved workers who picked grapes. The owner of the vineyard went to the town center early in the morning to hire men to help him pick grapes. He found some workers available and he hired them for a fair days wage and sent them to work. Then he went back to the town center at noon and found others available and hired them too for a fair wage. Then he went to the town center late in the afternoon and hired more men.

At the end of the day, he paid the men who worked all day their fair wage. But then he gave all the other workers the same amount even though some had worked only a short time. Those who worked all day in the hot sun complained it was not fair to give everyone the same. The owner answered and said he gave them all a fair wage just like he promised.

In the story, the vineyard owner symbolizes God. It was not fair to give all the workers the same wage, those who complained were right. Some had worked long hours and others just a short time yet they all got the same pay. But the owner realized that all the men had families to support with kids at home, so he gave them all a full day's pay. This is the way God takes care of us. It doesn't seem fair yet there is great love and concern for all in the way God deals with people.

# CHAPTER 13
# EACH PERSON NEEDS A DEEP SPIRITUALITY

Remember how Jesus told His apostles and disciples to wait in Jerusalem until the Holy Spirit comes on them. Only then could they go out and share the good news. He knew they couldn't do it without the help of the Spirit. That force and great power for evangelization comes mainly from the Holy Spirit. We all must have the Holy Spirit deep within our hearts to be effective in building the kingdom of God here on earth.

Not only that, but we need the Holy Spirit to face the challenges that come before us each day and to guide us in what we do each day.

The nature of the deep spirituality varies with the individual. Jesus recommended the Holy Spirit to His apostles and disciples. Many good Christians have a great devotion to the third person of the Trinity. Some have a devotion to Mary, the earthly Mother of Jesus. She has a great influence on her Son as we know from the wedding feast at Cana. Mary is a special person conceived without sin and Jesus listens to her. Others may prefer a popular saint like St. Francis of Assisi. But some deep spirituality is needed for each of us. No matter how young or how old we are, we each should have a well-founded spiritual basis. Frequent reception of the sacraments is a great help.

# CHAPTER 14

# PRODIGAL SON

This proverb is about a farm family who worked very hard. They had two sons, many servants and many livestock. One day the younger son asked his father to give him his rightful share of the family's money. He wanted to go off on his own and to lead a different life. The father loved the son and wanted him to stay but gave him the money anyway. The son lived a wild life and wasted all his money. He then got a job working for another farmer taking care of pigs. He did not make much money and sometimes didn't have money to buy food for himself.

Finally, the younger son thought about his home, even the servants there had enough to eat. He said, here I am starving. He thought he should return home and ask his father to forgive him, and to take him back as one of the servants. The father's heart was filled with love when he saw his son coming back and ran out to greet him. The father hugged him and told his servants to bring the son some new clothes and a ring for his finger and also to prepare a celebration for the son who was lost but now is found.

When the older son returned, he asked one of the servants what was happening and was told that his younger brother had returned home and that they were having a party for him. The older son then went to his father and complained that he had never been given a party and yet had been faithful in working on the family farm. Now the younger brother who had wasted the family money was being celebrated. He himself who had worked hard for many years was being ignored.

There are two important principals illustrated in the story. The father represents God and shows how much He loved his family and how completely He forgave the younger son. He was happy to have him back. Also the Father told the older brother that he always loved him and deeply appreciated all his help on the farm. Furthermore the father said you are not going to be cheated, you will get your fair share. Everything I have is yours.

So if someone you know is doing much better than you are, don't be jealous and complain to God. Just keep trying to do your best and God will give you your just rewards.

# CHAPTER 15

# GOD RULES THE NATIONS

If there is a God, then Nations of the world that honor God should do well in the world. And Nations that don't honor God should not do so well in the world. There are two good examples of godly Nations which have done well, Israel and the USA, at least in its early years. Also there are two Nations that were not godly, Communist Russia and Communist China. Let's mention these examples.

Israel has been a godly Nation since the time of Abraham (2000 BC). They were taken care of in the time of famine when they lived with the Egyptians. Then God helped them escape slavery in Egypt. They became a prosperous and independent Nation which has lasted for about 3500 years. Twenty five percent of all the Nobel Prizes have been awarded to Jews. Yet Jews make up only about 0.2 percent of the world's population. They are very successful people.

The USA was established in 1776 as a godly Nation. It expanded rapidly to become the most powerful, most progressive Nation on the planet. It survived the Civil War by the grace of God who used Abraham Lincoln in a mighty way. However in recent years, the USA has become less godly, focusing on abortion and same sex marriage and is not as progressive as before.

On the other extreme, Communist Russia abolished many churches and turned them into warehouses in their part of the world. They thought Communism was important but that "religion was opium for the people". About two million people lost their lives in Communist Russia. In China, a similar situation

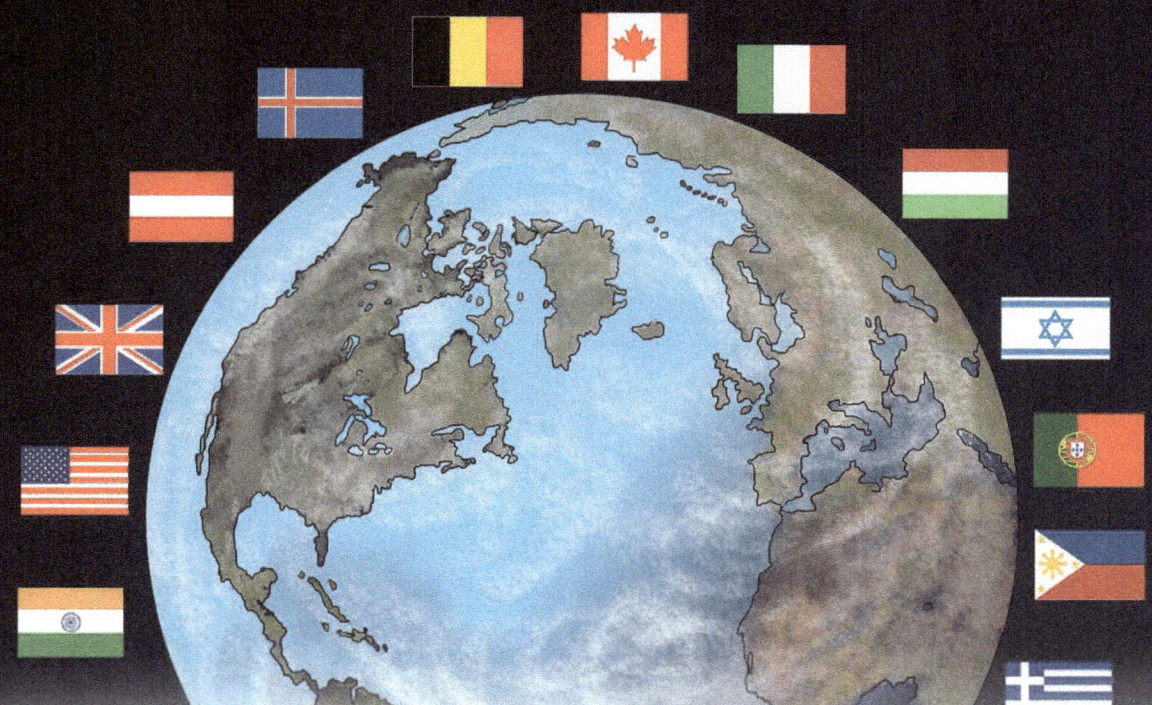

occurred and about twenty million people lost their lives. It appears that God is essential for governments to function well.

We need to mention Joan of Arc whom God called to save the Country of France from the invading British Army. They were at war for many years. In about the year 1430 Joan of Arc was praying and got the idea that God wanted her to save her country by leading an army against the British who had surrounded the city of Orleans. When she mentioned it to the governor, he laughed at her. He couldn't imagine a 17 year old girl leading an army, but when he thought about it, he decided to give her a chance. She freed the city of Orleans and went on to help free her country from the British Army. She is the "Patron Saint of France". It appears that when Nations turn to God, they are blessed and become successful but when they turn away from Him, they falter.

# CHAPTER 16
# DRUGS AND FAMILIES

Pharmacology is the study of drugs. When they are used correctly, they can do wonders and lives are saved. Pharmacology, physiology and pathology are said to form the basis of clinical medicine. To understand pharmacology, a doctor must have a good knowledge of physiology (absorption of food, urine formation, nerve and muscle function) and pathology (what happens when diseases alter physiology).

Drugs usually act on "receptors" in cells of the body. The receptors then produce desired changes to correct body function. However some drugs actually block receptors for chemicals made in the body when these chemicals are made in excess. Ideally, drugs do whatever is necessary to restore body function to normal.

Sometimes drugs act on their receptors but also act on other things in the body to cause "side-effects". A good example is propranolol. It is used to block receptors in the heart in patients with high blood pressure. This drug also increases fluidity of cell membranes in the brain and alters brain receptor function. One patient was taking propranolol to correct his high blood pressure but the drug also altered brain receptor function and changed his behavior. He divorced his wife. She really loved him so it was a sad family situation.

Some drugs are not used for therapy but rather for the pleasurable sensations they produce. Many family problems and much heartache are associated with misuse of these drugs. Last year, the leading cause of death for people under age fifty was not cancer or heart disease or motor accidents, but drugs! We have a huge problem killing 59,000 people with drugs like heroin, cocaine, opioids and the new fentanyls in 2016.

Ethanol has been a problem for families for decades. It causes severe addiction in about eight percent of its users. Men lose their jobs, families are disrupted, mental retardation occurs in infants born of alcoholic mothers, and alcoholic liver cirrhosis is common. Many addicted alcoholics die of the disease. There are no effective drugs for treatment of alcohol addiction. Also psychologists are not very helpful in treating the disease.

Yet some believe that because it is legal, alcohol will cause no harm. We have so many boring meetings to attend in our jobs and in our communities. They think alcohol is needed to loosen people up.

The only effective, dependable treatment for severe alcohol addiction is Alcoholics Anonymous. In its twelve step program, one step is belief in a higher power. Only when these people admit they are helpless against this powerful addiction and need God's help, can they successfully deal with the problem.

Marijuana is another serious drug problem. Twenty nine States in the USA plus the District of Columbia have laws which broadly legalize marijuana as of the year 2017. Ten percent of marijuana users become addicted and this leads to abuse of ethanol and heroin.

Marijuana abuse is widespread with 181 million users world-wide compared to only 33 million users of amphetamine. We are going in the wrong direction by legalizing addictive drugs. Family violence is enhanced by alcohol and substance abuse. Marijuana is the most commonly identified illegal drug in deadly car crashes. The combination of marijuana and even small amounts of ethanol is even more dangerous.

Our brains have 12 billion neurons and are finely- tuned instruments. When brains are exposed to drugs, they disrupt the fine balance there and cause unwanted changes in our normal selves. God created us with a perfect balance of neurotransmitters and receptors. Drugs can disrupt that balance.

Anxiety, anger, boredom and depression are common reasons why people abuse drugs. We need God's consolation/protection and not marijuana or alcohol to treat these conditions.

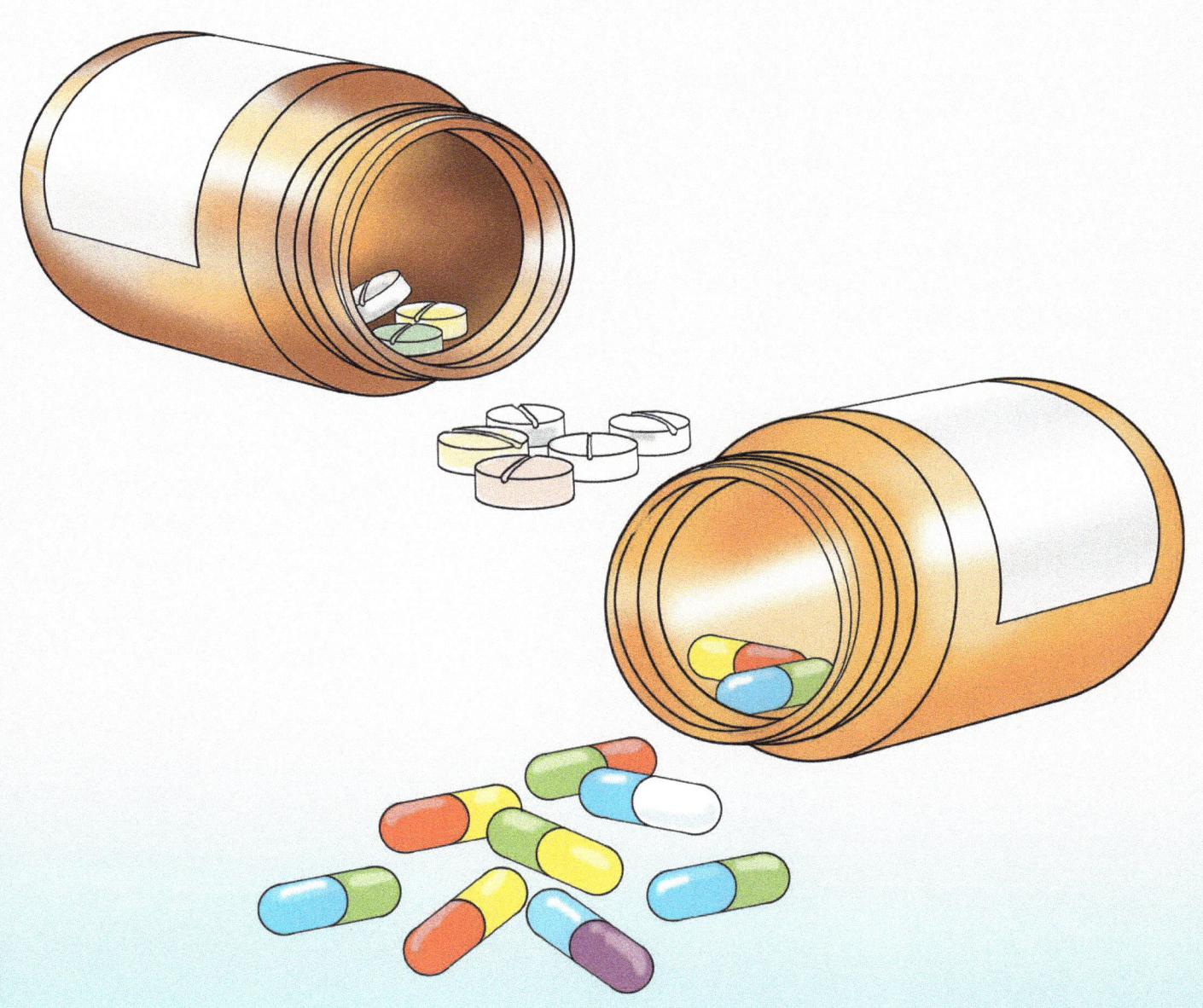

# CHAPTER 17
# FAMILIES AND MENTAL ILLNESS

Mental illness is common in human societies. It is evenly distributed around the world. It afflicts about twenty percent of the population, although only a half of one percent is actually diagnosed with schizophrenia. Symptoms grow worse with time. Families that have schizophrenic children must take care of them since they cannot care for themselves. It can be a great burden on many families.

Schizophrenics have disorganized thinking and speech (word salad), social withdrawal, loss of motivation and judgment and sometimes paranoia or hoarding of useless things. When they are older they continue to have poor hygiene, don't shave, don't have their hair cut or trim their nails and don't care for their homes.

Schizophrenia has both positive and negative symptoms. Disordered thoughts and speech and also visual hallucinations are positive symptoms that respond well to drug therapy. Negative symptoms include lack of emotion, poverty of speech, inability to experience pleasure (anhedonia), and lack of desire to form relationships. Negative symptoms do not respond well to drug therapy and are more of a burden to other people.

Deficits occur in attention and memory in the mentally ill more so than in normal people. Healthy people remember positive words better (Polyanna principle). Schizophrenics remember all words equally well and are at a disadvantage.

Providing instruction for these people improves function. Training emphasizes repeated verbalization of tasks and giving encouraging coping instructions to themselves. In other words, they are just like the rest of us, they have to work at it and keep a positive attitude to accomplish anything.

When the first antipsychotic drug, chlorpromazine, came out in the mid-1950s, many mental health hospitals built the previous seventy five years were closed. Using this drug allowed schizophrenics to leave the rigid confines of an asylum and return to the comfort of their own homes and communities. What a blessing this drug was to many members of our society.

Side effects are always a concern when drugs are used. These antipsychotic drugs may cause stiff motor movements in walking. Quetiapine (Seroquel) causes less abnormal motor movements but may cause some weight gain and diabetic symptoms.

Xavier Amador, a Ph.D. in psychology wrote a book "I am not sick, I don't need help" (1150 Smith Road, Peconic, New York, Vida Press, 2000). A revision of the first book came out in 2011. These books have revolutionized treatment of schizophrenia. Because of abnormal nerve tracts in their brains, these patients feel healthy (anosognosia), but they are not. It's a challenge to get them to take their medication because they think they are not sick.

Therapists have learned to befriend these patients and help them realize how important it is to take their medication as recommended. This prevents further deterioration of the disease state.

Caffeine addiction is common in schizophrenia. Incidence of cigarette smoking in the normal population is about twenty percent and increases to eighty five percent in schizophrenia. Living in an urban environment doubles the incidence of schizophrenia. Regular exercise has a positive effect on mental illness whereas use of marijuana increases the incidence of schizophrenia two to three times. Suicide occurs in five percent of these people. Schizophrenia decreases life span by ten to twenty five years.

We said chlorpromazine was a great blessing allowing patients to be reintegrated into their own families and to be freed from the confines of an asylum. The discovery that this drug slows worsening of schizophrenic symptoms was another amazing scientific advance. Now we are called to urge these patients to be diligent in taking their medication so they can maintain their level of sanity. We also need to encourage these people to be as productive as possible in society.

## CHAPTER 18
# IMPORTANCE OF SMALL PRAYER GROUPS

In the early church, small groups of believers would meet, sometimes in each other's homes, to encourage and to inspire one another with the help of the Holy Spirit. Like St. Paul, they had the sufferings of Christ as their central focus. They appreciated the great sacrifice that the good Lord made for all mankind. Many believe that there is also a great need in Christian Churches today for small, fervent prayer groups to meet to provide support and fellowship.

Our churches have grown so large that individuals get lost in the crowds. Also services sometimes become ritualistic and impersonal. We need that deep spirituality of small prayer groups to help us to love one another, to be ourselves and to be in good fellowship with one another.

It is said that without the help of the Holy Spirit, Christianity would not have lasted for over two thousand years. So often people get distracted by our noisy modern society, they lose the ability to concentrate. So we need these small prayer groups to isolate ourselves in a quiet place to feel the presence of the Holy Spirit, and consider serious, godly concepts. We need to become fully aware of the great majesty of our Lord and concentrate on Him alone. Some believe small prayer groups will become not only the lifeblood of the church but the hope for the future of our whole society.

No matter how old you are, you need a deep, close, spiritual relationship with other people. You're not a well-rounded person without these things. Some families gather each day for prayer. This is especially needed if you're very young or very old. Others may gather with people at work over the lunch-break. Many churches have prayer groups which meet regularly. It is a great joy to fellowship with other deep believers to honor the Lord who made us.